THE KNOPF POETRY SERIES

The
Unlovely
Child

# The

# Unlovely

# Child

*poems by*

# Norman Williams

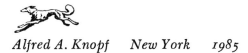

*Alfred A. Knopf    New York    1985*

THIS IS A BORZOI BOOK
PUBLISHED BY ALFRED A. KNOPF, INC.

Copyright © 1984 by Norman Williams
Published in the United States by Alfred A. Knopf, Inc.,
New York, and simultaneously in Canada by Random House
of Canada Limited, Toronto.
Distributed by Random House, Inc., New York.

"The Tremors at Balvano" was originally published in the
*Georgia Review.* "Clam Flats off Wales: A Theory," "For a Girl
Walking the Fields of Michigan in Mourning," and "Low
Clouds at Evening off Nova Scotia" were first published in
*Harvard Magazine.* "First Skaters, Perkins Pier" first appeared in
*New Criterion.* "The Birth of the Miraculous Child," "Ancient
Rites and Mysteries," and "The Dream of South" were first
published in *The New Yorker.*

Library of Congress Cataloging in Publication Data

Williams, Norman.
     The unlovely child.

     I. Title.
PS3573.I45515U5   1985   811'.54   84-47908
ISBN 0-394-53770-X
ISBN 0-394-72763-0 (pbk.)

Manufactured in the United States of America

FIRST EDITION

# Contents

The
Unlovely
Child

# The Birth of the Miraculous Child

In the dark morning when most children are born,
When only a few all-night lights star the prairie
And the east shifts slowly from black to blue,
When farm wives have their worst and most accurate dreams,
The girl in danger inside the only bright house
Believes with all her strength there are in the sky
Planets crossing, and an old woman in town
Starts in her bed, and, indeed, the next day,
When others shuffle along the dry road
To drop gifts and glimpse the miracle,
They remark that this at last might be
The child born at God's order for purposes other
Than riding the fields all day, than drinking
And coming for them at the very worst moment,
That this at last might be a man to free whores
And teach men to cherish something other
Than grudges, to show them, in short,
That there is more to life on this earth
Than the price of sides and cattle feed . . .
But no, he too baits the Negro boys,
Gulps whisky on long summer days, and,
Growing old, spends his time gambling—
Or so I imagine it must have been
For him to tell of the hours one day
He spent at the sink when his mother
Told him of the mark of innocence on his face.

# Giants of the Midwest

I have seen them in their plaid shirts and high boots
Carrying five clattering pails at evening back from the barn,
Casting huge shadows, and have watched them in wonder
At night in the switchyards calling out to the engines
In thundering tones, waving red flares in broad arcs,
And I have seen their goat-faced young, already gigantic,
On the football fields cracking hard against one another,
Lost in their November breath, and have also studied
The old ones, obese on back stoops, their swaybacked homes
Left like great mastodons on the prairie. Grandfather,
With his momentous limp and furuncled nose,
With his sure eye for the legs of horses and women,
Once walked among them, a colossus of the Depression
Who grew large knocking door-to-door across the Midwest
For any available work, including the hauling of offal,
Septic dredging, and other positions involving manure.
He subsisted, in those lean years, mainly on the shock
He felt when his wife, like the market, was seized
By contractions and shortly thereafter collapsed.
At last, several days before turning sixty,
He abandoned his legendary past
For the culverts and curbs of Maxwell Street, there
Overcoming his lifelong fear of God,
Turning up dead drunk beneath a folded paper,
His bloated trunk requiring six hands to hoist it,
An outsized casket, and a grave you could get lost in.

# Seagulls Above Kansas

As grandmother, hearing shot and ankle huge
With the storm-dark shades of gangrene,
Lay waiting for her death, she gathered us
One evening and described the day when,
As a child, she had seen above the Kansas fields
A group of gulls crying like children strayed,
And, in telling this, spoke in such strange tones
As if to show, because of it, her stinted life
Had not lacked for miracle. A few days later,
When she began to hunt the sheets and piled quilts
For air, then ceased at all to twitch or stir,
I saw the birds again, crouched on posts
And peaks of roofs, following a tractor
In raucous celebration as it turned a field,
Or rising with the sound of riffled books.
Like some new band of immigrants, the gulls
Were common now, and took the lowest work,
And yet, like her, one wondered as one watched
Their feints or giant swings, if they could ever
Fit themselves to this bare region of the earth.

# The Genius of Small-town America

Here our fathers stopped their westward push,
Not, God knows, for love of scenery or soil,
But because an ox gave out, an axle broke,
Or a child took with cholera or chills.
Now, their sons cross the fields like roofwalkers,
Chucking dirtclods at the crows, while in the shade
The women mutter of lost limbs and hopes.
Like a periodic curse, a drought this month
Has once more settled on the western plains,
Thickening the creeks, working into wayside barns,
And famishing the stock. On kitchen radios
One hears again the pulpit-pounding talk
And familiar promises of punishment,
That we have ourselves to blame for this,
Who lusted, craved and coveted—
But if sin lingers in these washed-up towns,
It could be only pride or stubbornness:
Each spring another crop of debt is sown,
And, though agencies attach the land,
Outbuildings, crops and unborn young, still
The beak-nosed men walk head-up and proud,
Convinced, against all evidence, that what
They've planted, built or reared is theirs,
And that, come the plague or Democrats,
They will die as they have lived, that is
In their good time, just when and how they choose.

# The Length of Midwestern Twilight

Within this endless epilogue,
When the scent of alfalfa mingles with
The odor of cows and casseroles,
Between the hour the thunderheads
Redden with the backlight of Asian dawn
And the moment that Venus shows
Dimly at last in the southwestern sky,
There is time on the Kansas prairie sufficient
For a girl to persuade another Four H-er,
And still for the boy, nearly struck dumb,
To hightail it back for the chores,
And, by the crossroads, there is time, too,
For an idiot unpotting shovels of earth
To see to completion his full inspiration—
This half-light encloses all of creation
For matted infants still damp from birth
And lends a depth to the failing view
Of invalids shut behind oaken doors
Within the huge and unstirring homes.
The dusk insinuates into the features
Of each fallen barn and settlement
Of feed lots and pumps that one passes by—
In the country, women gather in clothes
In light left after the sun is gone;
Their men, gnat-small on dusty roads,
Walk the long horizon at nightfall
Until nothing remains but the breath
Of junkfire, and distant barking of dogs.

# Mrs. Nietfeldt Alone at Midnight

Each spring, boulders surface in the fields
Like the bodies of drowned sailors.
The boundary posts, like tilting guards,
Keep out what never wanted in.
Alone thirty years, I think of the summer
My husband, harvesting corn, dried to a stone
In the sun. I think, too, of a black snake
Wrapped in the cellar like a bad dream.

At twilight, the stone wall glows
With the warmth of hands that set it.
An owl's wings beat across the barnyard
With the sound of heavy breathing. A woman
Whose hands have shrunk to sparrow's claws,
I close my eyes and see blank-faced men
Who've had a nightmare so full of terror
Nothing else can ever matter. I imagine
Women who placed love ahead of life
Dropping from windows late at night.

Newspapers from miles away blow up
Against the west side of the barn
With notices of births and deaths
That, years ago, I missed . . .

Sometimes, at night, I wake up suddenly,
As if the center of a storm had passed
Directly through the empty room.
The moon washes my walls the color of bone,
And the buzzing crickets grow suddenly loud.

# The Smelt Fishers

Still, tonight, in later spring,
The midwest poor, the city blacks
And rural whites, pitch their tarps
Among the square-cut stones that form
The western shore of Lake Michigan,
And as the first green insects buzz
And stumble in the air, these laggards
Deal their cards by lantern light,
Waiting the way that they have waited
Through the long Chicago winters
On listing wharves for bottomfeeders,
Or huddled in the stovepiped huts
That fill the marshes of Wisconsin;
Wait the way that they have waited
All their lives for that one break,
Through long illnesses of parents
Or at the bearing of their children:
Here, this evening, where the slab
Edges to the newly melted water,
Beneath a rising, blooded moon,
For the silent, silver running.

# Houses in Dunes Acres

Deep and forgotten in the forests here,
The summer remains of the twenties' rich
Crouch like lions on stuccoed haunches.
Each morning, again, comes dappled sunlight
And the twittering of birds. Shades
Of favored servants still deliver tea and Danish
To the master bedroom, and the faded paper
Reports a rally based on Hoover's latest speech.
Outside two guests resume a tennis match,
Neither able to win two-up. A lepidopterist
Once more pursues a Mourning Cloak, while
In the pool two lovers green and harden
With the turn of seasons. A month or more
My friend and I have ripped down lattice work
With which to roast the slow, fat hares
That push through the overgrown French garden . . .
At evening, fingering some moldering edition
From the walnut shelf—Adam Smith or Alger—
One recalls that late October afternoon
When trucks came piling down the gravel drives
To board the flues and windows after, all day,
The rotund brokers tumbled from their offices
Like apples in an autumn breeze. Apparently,
They had never lived in ruined houses
And, by their graphs, could not conceive
A life like ours being worth their while.

# For a Girl Walking the Fields
# of Michigan in Mourning

The girl walks with one knee almost stiff,
The way her father taught her, the way his father walked.
For generations now the family has moved as if
It were not yet accustomed to this earth.
Behind the haze the late March sun
Spreads along a distant bank of trees;
Water lies between the broken rows
Of corn, like wreckage at a battleground.
She thinks of her grandfather's collapse,
Magnificent, a plowhorse in the sun,
Nostrils flaring and sweat pouring off his back,
And remembers, too, the morning condensation
Beading on her window, like his final breath . . .
Behind her, in the distance now, the farmhouse
Resembles a full-masted ship edging off the world.
Soon the windows would be nailed shut,
And, near the workshed, mice would nest
Beneath the harrow he never quite got fixed.
Ahead, two robins toss a worm in flight;
This spring the worms lay gorged and drunken on the fields
As if, again, winter had been too generous.

# Those Crabapples

Thinking, at first, to try a jam,
I gathered them in two's and three's
Like toy bolas from the wayside grass
And, spilling from my folded shirt,
Carried them a long way back.
Hard and undelicious, they were
Once the only fruit that grew
In my midwestern neighborhood
And, as such, much favored in
Children's wars and sometimes, too,
On certain chilly Saturdays,
In steaming kitchens boiled down
Into a marmalade which,
Like most, wasn't really good—
But that was childhood, and so,
Once home, I dumped my pick
Carefully into a bowl and let
Its faint, ripe odor fill the room.

# For Melissa in Her Finery

I sit among my sister's fine and private things,
A shelf of English dolls, envelopes with fancy seals,
Rounded stones collected at a beach last spring,
And feel the way an amnesiac, perhaps, would feel,
Passing faces that once he could have known
Or walking unmarked streets that, as in a dream,
Break off in vacant squares or unfamiliar zones.
Older, I know some of what my sister's seen,
Father's start, and our mother's slow unhinging,
Yet, sitting at her cluttered desk, can only guess
The odd particulars of her days and evenings,
Which is her favorite author, special dress,
The songs she plays on her recorder, and, at night,
Which stone she fingers as she writes her journal:
"Often now," she'd entered, "I read until first light,
And think myself a rodent, wide-eyed and nocturnal."
The sentimental are those who've borne the most
And, as a child would, ask now to bear no more.
Before I leave, I'll walk up and down the coast
For stones or, better, find for her an antique store
With English dolls, each breakable and ancient,
With a bearing like her own: still, close-lipped, and patient.

# Learning to Whistle

At once, the breath, the lips, the tongue:
Something which, or said my father,
As he larked it in garage and cellar,
Could not be taught but had to be
Discovered, each man for himself,
And so, just four, I bundled in
A kitchen corner, before anyone
Was up, and in the church-weak light
Of winter, blew until light-headed.
For lisping months I carried on,
Until, one day taking me aside,
My mother told me in her house
One whistler was enough. But now
I have reached my father's age
And, astonished, find myself
With his odd eye and thinning hair—
At times, too, I try once more
For what was then beyond my reach:
Mostly still the sibilants, but then,
Too, ever so occasionally, a tone.

# The Moment Out of Time

It was a mix-up, the flutist now recalls,
Landing in this studio with windows like a cell,
Reminding her, in its claustral stillness
And in its must of yellowed texts, of all
Those rooms in which she'd spent her illness,
Running scales and trilling half the day,
Concentrating on her timbre—mother
In that time gave maybe too much love or praise,
Listening each afternoon that winter
As, outside, the park and boulevards grew dark—
Then mother died, instead. . . . Now, slowly,
The season turns to winter, and the light
Of five p.m. declines. . . . She wonders, suddenly,
How her mother's leg might sound—
Flutes were once carved of bone—
For her, each note and register is ground
In sickness, in mother rocking all alone,
Turning once to show an illustration
From a book of Dickens: a Coketown boy
Who, by his look, knew his situation
Worsening. . . . Why did I shun father's toys
At Christmas, the company of others, sex?
What woman, tending frozen peas and infants,
Isn't better off? But she corrects
The music, bewildered at these sentiments—
Recups the flute, expels a breath, forgets.

# Skonoke's Barber Chair

Set among the saloon rows
Of tonics, barbicides and ointments,
It was an old and proper throne,
A chair fit for a fireman,
Decked with all the gadgetry
The twenties had to offer—
The sterling, waffle-iron footrest
Embossed proudly by its local maker
And the black-knobbed, elbowed lever
That sent, like some Big Bertha,
The whole contraption skywards.

For twenty-some-odd years there now,
I had ordered up the sideburns
And D.A.'s of a slicked-back youth,
Trundled down as regular as church
Each Saturday to take my place
On that plush red leather, grimed
By the backside printer's ink
Of its patrons from across the street,
War-greased men in newsprint hats,
A tribe to which the family belonged,
My grandfather, whose mind is gone,
Who wanders, aimlessly and muttering,
As though his head were bucketed,

And father, lamed in some close shave,
Who limps and clatters on behind.

The press these last ten years has been
Draped in polyurethane, the cause
The union and main bearings shot.
The regulars, or most, have drifted off,
And now, this early autumn Saturday,
Some six of us alone sit round
Listening to the high school game,
Two customers, and the others come
To remark our local politics,
Who this year will pluck that plum
Of raking up Kiwanis Park, and then
Word of some variance allowing in
A dentist up near Mackler's Place—

"Better jawsmith than headbutcher,"
Now croaks old Mackler from the chair,
And, eyeing him, I think a moment
Of an oldtime silent comedy, based,
Must be, on that Depression saw,
"A drunken barber shaves the world,"
In which our hero finds himself
Next up at a barber's school

While, ahead, a poor bewhiskered soul
Loses not just muff and thatch
But nearly ears as well, and yet,
When our timid hero's turn arrives,
He steps up, albeit diffident,
Because, well, it seems polite—
Would I likewise? Of course not, no,
But now the barber ruffs the bib
And, catching me at daydreams,
Deeply bows and shows the chair
With a flourish, elaborate and grand:
I would—timorous, hesitant—I am.

# The Family Jewels

My father was the sort of man mothers warn
Their daughters of, a Socialist and Christian
Who could explain neither his politics nor religion.
I remember him, unshaven, hauling off in the dark
Of Sunday mornings to hawk papers beneath the elevated.
I think, too, of how his scraped and sinewed hands
Would fly up with a sudden violence,
Like peregrines uncloaked and loosed upon
Some hapless, unsuspecting prey. This winter,
On a hill in Massachusetts with white rocks
Littered like so many skulls, I found his grave,
Small and neglected, as befits a man who gave
His life and greater thought to drink. Near it
Were the woods and gullies where I spent my youth,
A shallow creek I lay beside, once, with a girl
While two muskrats nosed the bank for food. Now,
In the snow, black ash scrape their rough-barked limbs,
And a rodent's corpse lies frozen on the bank.
Small and neglected, these hands are all my legacy:
They too have rubbed against the northeast cold
And gripped themselves in fervent prayer. Holding
A shaking cigarette, I watch them twitch and start
Like hatchet men, waiting for an opening.

# Notes from the
# Secret Lives of Objects

### *I.*

We noticed it as children, first, on that day
When the senses quickened, and what had seemed
An underwater world, full of shadowplay
And sounds like humming transformers, redeemed
Itself with full particulars and clarity—
I mean, the sheer variety of objects,
The pull-toy dachshund, always in the nursery,
With its flapping jaw and profundo voicebox;
Or downstairs, the oriental figurines
That danced or shyly turned behind their fans
Within the china cabinet; or, finally,
Outside, the iridescent blue and green
Wings of the dragonfly, the leggy span
Of harvest flies, and spinning maple keys.

### *II.*

We viewed each new discovery, each bloom,
Unclaimed galosh, or unhinged freezer door
With gravity and circumspection, like flotsam
Tossed up on a beach the night before
For our delectation, without a past
And subject to our stringent tests of feel,
Taste and smell. In this way, we came to know
The scent of empty cellars, the biting taste
Of copper coin and prurient appeal
Of trunks with petticoats and satin bows,

Yet did not guess that certain articles
Were all the while capturing events,
That father's pipe would serve as chronicle
Or mother's quilt become her monument.

### III.

Now, once more, we climb the attic stairs
On this final visit home, to rummage chests
And hatboxes for a keepsake or a souvenir—
A watch or mantel clock in disrepair,
Some tankard blazoned with the family crest,
Or a tiepin, maybe, out-of-style forty years.
Then, like persecuted Jews with gunny sacks
And poor, dilapidated mules, we bundle them
For travel, knowing that we won't be back—
It is as though the house had been condemned,
The stock turned out and fields burned, and we alone
Sent off by night to find some better land
Where we might marry, root, and carry on,
Remembering by odd bits and scattered ends.

# The World Is on Fire

Railing by night through the prairie heat
I hear the bones of Kansas towns crack.
In a Grand Hotel a rafter gives way;
A wall collapses in a Bijou Marquee . . .
Nebraska cafes and Burlington shacks
Bleach like cattle skulls the next day.
From the tracks behind ghosts swelter up:
I remember father at night in the dome car
Pointing out stars to me and my mother;
I remember their tipsy fights in the club
And them necking behind the meatpacking yards.
Now the fields redden with Canadian bur;
Weather grays storefronts, and slowly,
Like snow in the sun, lives gather in—
The same shrunken people wander each village:
Father, on the courtsteps, cracks open wheat,
While mother, in our white Victorian kitchen,
Mutters and storms, breaking her china in rage.

# The Spare Room

For thirty years, almost, we've traded dreams,
My father's of leading me, small and baseball-capped,
Down an unpaved country road toward Death,
And mine of one day standing next to him
While the timbers of the house collapsed—
Some weeks ago, like an old and shuffling dog,
He took residence downstairs, and now lies evenings
Neither sleeping nor awake, his chest heaving up and slackening
With the rattle of a sea in which a ship has wrecked.

These fissured plains were sea-floor once,
And from their muddy flats emerged
Those first strange forms to try the earth—
And it was here, in our later Cenozoic,
The prairie schooners pulled up short,
And through long, cloudless summer days
Unshipped their ploughs and tableware.
I picture them, our dismounting forefathers,
As stern and leather-faced as tortoises,
And see my beak-nosed father, in his age,
At sea among the waves of cattle corn and wheat.

It is as though this windswept land itself
Beat back each new life that settled it—
Tonight, its scent of grass and spread manure
Seeps from the space beneath the door,

From the casement and creases of my father's skin,
And I wonder, breathing it, if he dreams as I do
Of the leaning houses tethered on the plains
By two twined cords, the phone and electricity,
Of the closed-up villages huddled by the rail spurs,
And of that long line, the bioblasts and pioneers,
That, before us, kept these landscapes that we share.

# Quidnunc

Bowed before my desk,
I find a glancing eye attracted
By the worn brass knob of the bedroom door,
My cheeks and lower jaw reflected
Oddly there, grotesque
And malproportioned, as in a funhouse mirror
Or a richly jeweled, polished spoon
Served with evening coffee—
The swollen shapes suggest another birth
And circumstance, a picaroon,
Perhaps, with bulging eye, or a nob of worth
And doubtful pedigree.
Still tilting my head, parrot-wise,
I recall another home, a parsonage
Of stately furnishings and size,
Whose passageways and pantries set the stage
For schemes and counterplots
In my young and fertile thought,
And realize that it was there,
While awaiting ham and currant pudding,
That I felt the first desire
To alter my appearance. On chairs
Pulled to a parlor fire,
My parents touched upon their hasty wedding
And later woes with the minister,
While I pretended not to hear.

Back then, I had not begun to guess
My role in the incident,
Yet must have had some hint
Of the alterative power I possessed.

# Forerunners

In bud-time, as the first few tufts
Of cotton appeared upon the willows,
I made my way upland from the swamp,
Having cut some switches for a friend
In hospital, whose odds were lengthening—
Spring rain all day had warmed the earth,
And now, at evening, a mist
Crept toward the higher ground.
Above ravines, there seemed to hang
The swollen hands of mendicants,
And, across the tablelands, the view
Recalled a formal banquet leavings,
The light refracted and diffused,
And the crusts of winter stacked beside
The gravel roads and thawing fields.

According to a farmer's superstition,
One may know a coming season
By certain days which run before,
And so, tonight, the mists and fog
Seemed special envoys of the fall
Forced, before their time, from earth—
As I recrossed the stiffened ground,
I thought of starlings ushered back

By northern winds, and cornstalks,
Lately full, downed by autumn storms.
I knew that when this day returned
I would be choosing winter wood
And thinking, as I marked the larch
And thickened oak, of today,
When I first felt the summer's loss.

# 19th-Century Tool Chest
## Found in New Jersey

It had the unimpeachable odor of ancestral Bibles,
Antique dolls, or the undergarments of old women,
This oaken chest with its brass-embroidered latch,
Quarter-barrel lid, and rotting leather straps,
Found among the yellowed jars of a cobwebbed cellar
In New Jersey, the impressive winter residence
Of a woolly spider common to the hinter parts,
Where the grocer's specialty, behind a counter hung
With netted cheese, was sausages and scandal.
The trunk, inscribed by one John Hunt, born 18-9,
The same whose stone stands in an ill-kept corner
Of the churchyard by itself, without family or wife,
Contained the precise ratchets, planes, chisels,
Cloths, and sanding blocks of a master woodworker
Laid each in its spot, as if for formal dinner,
But in the place of honor, against a velvet back,
There fanned a circle of elegant French pistols,
Evidence of his private hobby, him whose portrait,
In enamel miniature, rattled on a lower shelf,
A man of upturned collars and a monocle who,
Without much trouble, could be imagined nights
By kerosene polishing the jewelled butts and steel,
Thinking of the man who was short with him that day
Or, perhaps, a woman who did not return his glance,

Although out here, two days by carriage from New York,
Away from commerce and the world, one would guess
His failure, like its smell, was thought, almost, respectable.

# Camping in the Blue Ridge

Weathered the color of old man's skin,
The abandoned cabins of Virginia
Lean like graves on the hillsides.
These are the leftovers of clans
With names like Ackerman or Clatterbuck,
Homesteaders who never quite believed
Ringworm would brand the cows each spring,
Or that forty acres of clay and stone
Would not keep the cellar in greens.
The fallen beams of the houses
Are cut from chestnut extinct fifty years.
The hand-fashioned spikes are the kind
On which martyrs once must have hung.
Studying the creases and folds of my hand,
The skin browned with tobacco and age,
I think of the hopes that someone,
Once, must have held out and wait
For the blood-warm night to settle in.

# West Tisbury, with Stars

With sudden hunger for the past, we set off
In the muggy haze of that late August day
To find the salt-eroded graves of sea captains
And whalers, with their odd names and epitaphs.
Heaved by a century of frost, the older stones
Told of infant deaths and childhood disease,
Of sailors lost and, by recurrent years,
Winters harder than the rest. Nearby churches,
Kept up for the tourist trade, proclaimed
By lack of furnishings and straight-backed pews,
Their fear of God and luxury. That night,
At last, a cold front cleared the sky to stars,
And, standing out, we saw the constellations
That would have once informed the Quaker hands
Of latitude and hour. Climbing with our eyes,
We moved uncertainly along the Dipper's arm
From Mizar to Arcturus—moved, I thought,
As we had moved among those listing graves,
Uncertain of our place or creed, and yet,
As tourists, touched by what we could not reach.

# For the Anonymous Builder
## of a Graystone Farmhouse

*Isle LaMotte, Vt.*
*c. 1870*

Who marked this spot, miles out
From any town, hemmed half the year
By drifts and heaving slabs of ice,
Would not have been a happy man—
No, more likely that he beat his wife,
Gave worship to an obscure sect,
Or, if less far gone than that,
At any rate did not get on
With the common run of men.
And yet, in ordering these stones be cut
And hauled by skid across ten miles,
In sleeping in the backlot hut
Two years, or three, to supervise
How this house of his went up,
He showed a scruple such as comes
Only in extremity—
It may be his wife was lost
Or late fortune frittered through,
But here, in likely middle age,
He meant to make himself a start
And, in choosing blocks the shade
Of lowered winter cloud, in seeing
Each upright square and lintel flush,
Showed of what a man is capable—
Here, some grizzled habitant
A hundred years ago pulled in a breath

And with it knew to certainty
That in this spot he'd take his death;
Knew that, and bowed his dogged head
Then set his spade and broke the earth.

# First Skaters, Perkins Pier

With thaw and cold, the early winter snow lay
In brownish patches on the fields, inspected
By the crows, and though the olive-colored water
Still mushroomed up and mottled the center
Of our lake with obscure streaks and bruises,
They came that Sunday, after early worship,
With skates across their shoulders, and, lacing up,
Debated who should be first that year to try
The ice that nudged the pier and breakwater.
Nearby, dinghies leaned against a summer stand,
And, on the point, a lighthouse stood, mute
Until the spring. At last, three boys moved off,
Their shaky weight dispatching splits and groans
That, for a moment, stilled them in their tracks.
I turned, then, back to coffee and the newspaper,
But, glancing up, saw to my surprise and wonder
The harbor filled an hour later with the pirouettes
Of a dozen figure skaters, with wobbling children
Bundled up to twice their size, and the slap
And dash of a pick-up hockey match. All of it,
The smallness of the figures, the grayish sky
And snow that eddied low across the ice, recalled
That in our latitude miracles are not at hand
And one must learn to care for ordinary things:
The tufted sparrow, washed-out moon, or unlovely child.

# Low Clouds at Evening
## off Nova Scotia

Off the shore the milling gulls floated on the ocean drafts
Like white mustaches, and the leaping foam paused in mid-air
And turned its back, like an outlaw who, at last, is shot.
Such were our remarks as we came in sight of Neil's Harbor
And there, on the piled rocks before its beaten houses,
An old man stripping logs, quickly, as one would scale fish.
I thought of his wife, at home, the dishes done,
Lying in her room, the last light catching on a cross,
And walking, in her thoughts, along that rubble coast
Where, almost fifty years ago, in a spot long since
Buried by the rocks, she had first drawn down a man.
Enough. She had watched today, in the netted catch,
A mackerel, its color gone, flip hours after it was caught,
As if the air were not exactly poisonous, but just too thin;
And she remembered, also, how the aging hackmatack,
Weathered, mottled, peeled, put forth still a living branch,
Though, of course, as anyone would say, they were mostly dead.
But soon her husband would be back and climbing into bed.
Already, now, she smelled him—the wood, the fish, the sweat.
A few dim lights unrolled on the blackened water,
And the gulls eyed the surf as one would eye the enemy.
As we turned from that bare rock, and those huge,
        unbending pines,
It seemed odd that, after all, we should call it "beautiful."

# Notes on Saturday

Oyster catchers
Wedged low across
   The water;
A trickster's deck,
Black, then veering,
   Blizzard-white.

All afternoon
Great cloud stacks roiled
   From the ridge;
Huge smoke, one thought,
From some awesome
   Act of God.

Swift wind below
Misted the sea
   With warm breath:
"Hurry," it said,
Shooing the back
   Of its hand.

Lady fingers
Leisurely bent
   By the cove;
Unsteady *f*'s,
As, on a page,
   A child's script.

Women disguised
As blackbirds talked
  Wicked chat;
"Wit, wit," counseled
The sanderling,
  Stepping quick.

Without a word
Evening made its
  Presence felt;
Lights gathered flesh
While trees lost all
  Dimension.

Suddenly—as
Though in the dusk
  A crofter
Stepped to beat a
Rug—seawards thrashed
  A heron.

As from a trout,
Then, freshly caught
  And mouthing
Dumbly its last
Prayer, all color
  Left the clouds.

# Stirrings

## Crosshaven

*Ireland, 1979*

In the furze that banks the estuary,
As the tide backed out, and some few souls
Gathered to meet the evening ferry;
Down a quarter-mile from the knoll
That baldly caps the Irish town,
And just before the sun broke clear
Of changing clouds, a dullish brown
But incisively marked bird flushed near
My step, and its sudden thrash and swat
Froze the moment in my thought.

## Kritsa

*Crete, 1980*

Each day, for seeming weeks on end,
The clouds and latter rains descend.
The barely breathing sea edges
Up and back, while in the hills
The rough-cast, white-washed villages
And huts keep shuttered-up and still.
Only the spiked and common broom,
With its unerring sense of time,
Like votive candles in the gloom
Tips its tangled ends in yellow,
As though it recognized below
The pale goddess on her climb.

# The Irish Bull

By turns cantankerous or sweetly innocent, a cuss
You would have called him, sprawled like some
Middle Eastern pasha in the corner of his pen,
Flesh rolling from his gut, his leathered balls
Inviting poker shots. In his ruttish prime,
He had mounted each indifferent heifer's back
And, with a clenched and rigid concentration,
Guided his seed to its spot. Now, among the slate
That breaks and tilts in these burrin fields,
His offspring nose and switch with minds elsewhere,
Content in any weather. Saddled by the debts
And sideling barns left to him years ago,
The farmer, passing by, hurls epithets in brogue,
Yet, honoring tradition, calls the creature "Brendan,"
After his own father, and in that sly, backhanded,
Irish way, pays his respects to both of them.

# Clam Flats off Wales:
# A Theory

A girl of nine or ten, gangling and plain,
In a slicker and red dime-store boots,
Bent with her younger brother, hooded,
Patient, to the bare and puddled sea bottom
To dig clams on a dull and drizzling day,
The kind that one expects in Wales,
And, after foraging some minutes, found
A large and darker husk, perhaps an oyster
That had died, lost anchor, and drifted there,
Barnacled and bearded with a brownish weed.
She called out, then, in her native tongue
A remark which got them giggling, and at which
The boy clumped over, having concluded
Nothing would do but to break it open,
Though prying and stamping with a heel failed.
But, finally, the girl pulled her pocket keys,
And knifed until, at last, the mollusk gave:
Inside there lay its living belly, white
And taut, which quivered to her touch
And at which (though her brother right away
Went back to nosing in the flats) she seemed
To wonder, setting it in an honored spot
Among her piled catch. Perhaps, though young,
She was that age when children first
Suspect there may be certain, furtive things
Their parents have not chosen to reveal,

Because, at dusk, when their grizzled father
Tramped down to fetch them back to town,
She refused his callused hand and walked
The lamplit street sideways, instead, staring up
As though to guess what lay behind his seaman's face,
As though to guess, that is, if he too somehow
Were strangely different from what he seemed.

# The End of the Journey

In Ayrshire, above the shuttered market town,
Where, at bitters, the talk most nights still got around
To those ten acres, free and clear, and where,
Among the villagers, a man was even now
Counted by his word and his ability to plough
(Though, in a pinch, a knack at darts would do),
And where, too, the springtime picking of the stones
And the mowing still formed the corners of the year,
I came across a field of thistle, in brown
Instead of purple, and to one side a simple church
Of plank and stone, Calvinist in its severity,
Its pulpit Bible left to a text forbidding appetite,
And resting there, on a hewn and bare-boned pew,
Thought of the nameless founders of the place,
Those who from the gray and salt-hung air
Had caught the mold that formed the local ale,
Had worn the paths that, like a fisher's net,
Now lay spread across the bogs and heaths,
And one day, too, had cut and shouldered up
These massive beams, as though to warn that here,
Between this stone-filled earth and lowered sky,
One found the world exactly as it was,
And one must fear and worship it.

# Words for a Stone in Coventry, Circa 1941

Each afternoon at four through that rainy winter
The lights went down, as though the Germans,
Honing in on some fluorescent bathroom bulb
Or child's nightlight in the hall, would blast
To smithereens one's family and faithful dog,
Books, bungalow and all. And so without
The requisitioned coffee, tea or marmalade,
We listened in the darkness, taking hands,
While flares lit up the cranes and smelter stacks,
And the Luftwaffe brought news from the continent.
Toward spring, as crocuses once more unbent
Beside the blackened walls and fractured walks,
I thought back to Brighton at the summer holiday,
When Germans in striped body trunks would tug
Their future infantry, and our own young RAF'ers
Would tilt and dive among the rearing waves.
Red licorice, as I recall, was then the rage
Among our younger set, while off the coast
Each humid afternoon the thunderheads
Would light and boom like mortars lobbed,
But always, only, distantly.

# The Dream of South

I dream, now, of a dream vacation,
Of unpaved roads that reach to desert towns
Filled with children brown as pinecones,
With goats that rattle off acacia leaves,
And the simple faithful, plainly dressed
In black and white, who, on cool mornings,
Filter in to ornate churches to observe
The patron saints and obscure holy days,
Candlemas or Lammastide. It is a charm
Of travel, to walk among the butcher stalls
And fishmongers of a village as neglected
As one's own, and in dank passageways
To sense the loom of local history,
The martyr freed or foreign king turned back—
Then, afterward, in language one cannot pronounce,
To order coffee and, while waiting the eternity,
Imagine what a life here might be like—
The curate, maybe, who at appointed hours
In solemn comedy bisects the central plaza,
Knowing himself mocked, or the pale woman
Who shyly glances back, in a small apartment
With squeaking clothesline and tiny, filthy kitchen,
Whose love is such that, from time to time,
One could be lifted wholly from oneself.

# Changing Parts

*The Algarve, Portugal*

In the owlish, pre-dawn light, the fishermen
With few words tossed their nets and ropes aboard
While, above, the masts swung back and forth
Like metronomes, or crosses tilting to a dirge.
Hours later, when the sun had warmed the air,
The pensioned Germans and Britishers appeared
In open blouses and baggy pantaloons
And, with us, stooped for shells along the shore.
Spread across the sand, sea trumpets lay
Wrapped like small white mummies, and urchins
Danced like late Victorians in hoop skirts
Where the ebb brought down the coming waves.

Like tinkers at a seaside fair, as we passed
We sometimes paused to show or trade
Our finer wares: two conchs bought a starfish,
Depending on condition, and nautilus, of course,
Were dear. And then, as we walked farther on,
You began this game of changing parts,
Dragging, like the German we had met,
Your foot behind like some unruly dog or child,
And I too started in, with that uncontrolled
Sniffing seen in our friend, the Britisher—
And so adopting stoops and tics we carried on
Until, now some ways down, we stopped to watch
A fishing boat lumber, creaking, toward the shore.

There were three of them, a family of Portuguese
In homespuns stiff with oil, a boy and jowled man,
Then Grandfather, his features worn with salt and age,
And, astride the gunnel, as the old man clambered out,
He slipped, legs shot, and gave a half-apologetic snort.
I caught then, by chance and for a moment only,
The young boy's glance, and, in his quick eyes,
The depth and look of sudden fright. Turning, then,
Once more toward the shadowed beach, I saw
The pensioners like distant prophets on the sand
And, out beyond, a woman to her knees in surf,
Ear to a shell, transfixed, as though above
All that constant rush of sea, she heard the sound
Or voice that once had called the slug away—
Saw, that is, or in that instant seemed to see,
With that boy's foreign, swift, expanded sight.

# In the Presence
# of Strange Tongues

*Granada, Spain*

I had watched, among the vendors, wives and maids
That Tuesday mornings filled the Moorish courtyard
With extravagant displays of vegetables and dickering,
A frail Arab girl, in flip-flops and a dingy shawl,
Load sacks with assorted grains and fleshy bulbs.
She seemed, like me, a stranger to the tented stalls,
Sent off to search the muttonhead and squid
For that which seemed digestible. I learned,
Today, to my amazement, she had been watched
By other, keener eyes, and that, somehow,
She shared a secret language with the women
Of the place, when, edging up and interrupting,
She motioned for a persimmon, and an older vendor,
Smiling at my peevish look, spoke in rapid Spanish
A phrase which, with my lexicon, I later found
Meant neither "ladies first" nor "those pushy Arabs,"
But closer to: "The young one's great with child."

# The Tremors at Balvano

*December 6, 1980*

The animals, that day, behaved with odd foreboding;
The hens refused their coops, and disgruntled swine
Upset their trays and rooted up their pens—
Toward evening, as the cobbled streets grew thick
With Romeos decked out in their *abitos de sera*,
The lightbulb strings began to tilt, and rumblings
Filled the stairwells, galleries and porticos
Like muttered news of scandal. The earth then shook
As sharply as a horse's flank nagged by summer flies,
And stone stacked centuries ago, the church and hillside huts,
Came down. Throughout that long and grieving night,
The villagers, the wise-ass boys and drunkard men,
The sturdy wives whose furrowed faces seemed to map
The yellow land, pulled out barely breathing bodies
By the arms, and as they worked the word went out
Of various astonishments, of a skimming village clerk
Thrown before the local priest, who, before he died,
Humbly begged forgiveness, and of a girl trapped
Hours with her mother, who, in that close darkness,
Learned the riddle of her birth. At last, near dawn,
The spades and picks were set aside, and, once more,
The congregation gathered by the ruined church,
There to make an offering and recite their prayer,
And to remind themselves, again, of what the Jews
Had known: "That Heaven strikes with greatest sorrow
Whom It loves the most." And then, as benediction,

And with that piety one feels close to others' deaths,
There came the lighting of the candles, a modest rite
That in the midst of all those dead and given up,
And of the waste that lay across the nearby slopes,
Grew to seem a strange, discreet, and human act.

# Ancient Rites and Mysteries

In Florence, early, a stooped man moves down the alleys
Waiting for the rinds to be set out for the pigeons,
And, at dawn, swallows wheel from the eaves and campaniles
Crying out a call of pain peculiar to this city.
One thinks of the plague that moled through these cellars
Six centuries ago, and of the beggars that begot these beggars
Rolling off their women to shuffle past the merchants' doors.
Though a sculptor, here and there, may have succeeded
At converting their bald pain into a kind of sorrow,
It lives still, an heirloom of back rooms and old piazzas,
And is first cousin to a suffering I used to think
Belonged to the Midwest alone, where I grew up,
Observing its essential rules: that men edge off
Just when their help is needed most, and that
A person, almost always, will starve before abandon
The land and circumstances of his birth. But more,
I saw that in Florence, too, a woman in a dusty dress
Will sometimes lean against a door she's leaned against
A thousand times, watching her child chase balking chickens,
And with her darkened teeth will smile
The selfsame smile that I have seen and wondered at
Among the plywood shacks of Kankakee or Peotone.

A NOTE ON THE TYPE

This book was set on the Linotype in a type face called Basker-ville. The face is a facsimile reproduction of types cast from molds made for John Baskerville (1706–1775) from his designs. The punches for the revived Linotype Baskerville were cut under the supervision of the English printer George W. Jones. John Baskerville's original face was one of the forerunners of the type style known to printers as "modern face"—a "modern" of the period A.D. 1800.

Composed, printed and bound by
Heritage Printers, Inc.
Charlotte, North Carolina

Designed by Iris Weinstein